Samuel French Acting Edition

Boesman and Lena

A Play in Two Acts

by Athol Fugard

SAMUELFRENCH.COM   SAMUELFRENCH.CO.UK

MUSIC USE NOTE

Licensees are solely responsible for obtaining formal written permission from copyright owners to use copyrighted music in the performance of this play and are strongly cautioned to do so. If no such permission is obtained by the licensee, then the licensee must use only original music that the licensee owns and controls. Licensees are solely responsible and liable for all music clearances and shall indemnify the copyright owners of the play(s) and their licensing agent, Samuel French, against any costs, expenses, losses and liabilities arising from the use of music by licensees. Please contact the appropriate music licensing authority in your territory for the rights to any incidental music.

IMPORTANT BILLING AND CREDIT REQUIREMENTS

If you have obtained performance rights to this title, please refer to your licensing agreement for important billing and credit requirements.

BOESMAN AND LENA was given its American Premiere by Circle in the Square, Theodore Mann and Paul Libin in association with John Berry, on June 22, 1970, at the Circle in the Square Theatre, with the following cast:

BOESMAN .... *James Earl Jones*

LENA .... *Ruby Dee*

OLD AFRICAN .... *Zakes Mokae*

Directed by John Berry

Scenery designed by Karl Eigsti

Lighting by David F. Segal

Costumes by Margie Goldsmith

Production Stage Manager Jan Moerel

The entire action takes place in the mud flats of the river Swartkops, South Africa.

Boesman and Lena

ACT ONE

An empty stage.

*A coloured man—*BOESMAN—*walks on. Heavily burdened. On his back an old mattress and blanket, a
blackened paraffin tin, an apple box . . . these con-
tain a few simple cooking utensils, items of clothing,
etc., etc. With one hand he is dragging a piece of
corrugated iron. Barefoot, shapeless grey trousers
rolled up to just below the knee, an old shirt, faded
and torn sports-club blazer, cap on his head. He
chooses a spot, then drops the corrugated iron, gets
down his load and slumps to the ground beside it.
He has obviously walked very far. He waits.*

*After a few seconds a coloured woman—*LENA—*appears.
She is similarly burdened—no mattress though—and
carries her load on her head. As a result she walks
with characteristic stiff-necked rigidity. There is a
bundle of firewood under one arm. Also barefoot,
wearing one of those sad dresses that reduce the
body to an angular, gaunt cipher of poverty.*

*A life of hardship and dissipation obscures their ages, but
they are most probably in their fifties.*

BOESMAN *looks up slowly as* LENA *appears. He watches
her with a hard, cruel objectivity. He says nothing.
She has been reduced to a dumb, animallike sub-
mission by the weight of her burden and the long
walk behind them and in this condition almost*

misses him sitting to one side, propped up against his bundle. Realising she has passed him, she stops, but does not turn to face him in case they have to walk still further.

LENA. Here? (BOESMAN *clears his throat and spits. She waits a few seconds longer for a word from him, then turns slowly and joins him. The bundle of firewood falls to the ground. Her arms go up and with the last of her strength she gets her bundle down. Her relief as she does so is almost painful. She sits down slowly. For a few seconds she just rests, her head between her knees, breathing deeply. Then she stretches forward and works a finger between the toes of one of her feet. It comes away with a piece of mud. She looks at it, squashing it between her fingers.*) Mud! Swartkops! (*She now looks at the world around her for the first time—she knows it well—then still higher up, into the sky, searching for something.*) Too late now. (*Pause.*) No, there's one. (*She is obviously staring up at a bird. Softly . . .*) Bastard! (*She watches it for a few seconds longer, then scrambles to her feet and shakes her fist at it.*) Clear out, bastard!! (BOESMAN *watches her, then the bird, then* LENA *again. Her eyes follow it as it glides out of sight.*) So slowly . . . ! Must be a feeling, hey? Even your shadow so heavy you leave it on the ground. (*She sits down again, even more exhausted now by her outburst. She cleans the mud from between her other toes while she talks.*) Tomorrow they'll hang up there in the wind and laugh. We'll be in the mud. I hate them. (*She looks at* BOESMAN.) Why did you walk so hard? In a hurry to get here? Jesus, Boesman! What's here? This . . . (*The mud between her fingers.*) . . . and tomorrow. And that will be like this! Rot! This piece of world is rotten. Put down your foot and you're in it up to your knee. That last spell was hard. Against the wind. I thought you were never going to stop. Heavier and heavier. Every step. This afternoon heavier than this morning. This time heavier than last time. And there's other times coming. *"Vat jou goed en trek!"* Whiteman says, "Clear out!" *Eina!* (BOESMAN *is watching her with undisguised animosity and disgust.*) Remember the old times? Quick march! Even run . . . (*A little laugh.*) . . . when they chased us. Don't make trouble for us here, Boesman. I can't run anymore. Quiet hey! Get out the bottle, man, let's have a *dop*. (LENA *registers* BOESMAN'S *hard stare. She studies him in return.*) You're the hell-in. Don't look at me *ou ding*. Blame the whiteman. Bulldozer! (*Another laugh.*) *Ja!* You were happy this morning. "Push it over my *baas!*" *"Dankie Baas!"* "We're on our way!" It was funny, hey, Boesman! All the shanties flat. The poor people running around trying to save their things. You had a good laugh. And now? Here we sit. Just now it's dark, and Boesman's thinking about building another shanty. The world feels big when you sit like this. Not even a bush to make it your own size. Now's the time to laugh. This is also funny. Look at us! Boesman and Lena with the sky for a roof again. (*Pause . . .* BOESMAN *stares at her.*) What you waiting for?

BOESMAN. (*Shaking his head as he finally breaks his silence.*) Jesus, Lena! I'm telling you, the next time we walk . . .

LENA. Don't talk about that now, man.

BOESMAN. *The next time we walk!* . . .

LENA. Where?

BOESMAN. . . . I'll keep on walking. I'll walk and walk . . .

LENA. *Eina!*

BOESMAN. . . . until you're so bloody tired that when I stop you can't open your mouth!

LENA. It was almost that way today.

BOESMAN. Not a damn! Wasn't long enough. And I knew it. "When she puts down her bundle, she'll start her rubbish." You did.

LENA. Rubbish?

BOESMAN. That long turd of nonsense that comes out when you open your mouth!

LENA. What have I said? I'm tired! *Eina!* That's true. And you were happy this morning. That's also true.

BOESMAN. I'm still happy.

LENA. You happy now?

BOESMAN. (*Aggressively.*) I'm always happy.

LENA. (*Mirthless laughter, clapping her hands.*) *Ek se!* His backside in the Swartkops mud, but Boesman's happy. This is a new sort of happy, *ou ding.* The hell-in happy.

BOESMAN. Why shouldn't I be happy?

LENA. *Ja,* that's the way it is. When I want to cry, you want to laugh.

BOESMAN. Cry!

LENA. Something hurt. Wasn't just your fist.

BOESMAN. Snot and tears because the whiteman pushed over a rotten old shanty? That will be the day. He did me a favour. I was sick of it. So I laughed.

LENA. And now?

BOESMAN. Yes. You think I can't laugh now?

LENA. Don't be a bastard.

BOESMAN. You want to hear me?

LENA. NO!

BOESMAN. Then shut up, or you will! I'm a happy *Hotnot.* Laughing all the time . . . inside! I haven't stopped since this morning. You were a big joke then, and if you don't watch out you'll be a big joke now.

LENA. Big joke? Because I cried? No, Jesus, Boesman! It was too early in the morning to have your life kicked in again. Sitting there in the dust with pieces . . . bare assed! That's what it felt like! . . . and thinking of somewhere else again. Put your life on your head and walk, sister. Another day gone. Other people lived it. We tramped it into the ground. I haven't got so many left, Boesman.

BOESMAN. If your legs worked as hard as your tongue then we were here long ago.

LENA. It's not my fault.

BOESMAN. Then whose? Every few steps . . . "Rest a bit, Boesman." "I'm tired, Boesman."

LENA. Poor old Lena! Nobody feels sorry for her.

BOESMAN. You weren't resting.

LENA. I was.

BOESMAN. You lie.

LENA. What was I doing?

BOESMAN. You were looking for that *hond* of yours.

LENA. *Hond?* (*She remembers.*) Dog! *Haai!* Was it this morning?

BOESMAN. You almost twisted your head off you were looking behind you so much. You should have walked backwards today.

LENA. He might have followed me. Dogs smell footsteps.

BOESMAN. Follow you! You fancy yourself, hey?

LENA. Anyway you weren't in such a hurry yourself. You didn't even know where we were going.

BOESMAN. I did.

LENA. Swartkops?

BOESMAN. (*Emphatically.*) Here! Right here where I am.

LENA. No, Boesman. This time you lie.

BOESMAN. Don't say to me I lie! I'm not mix-up like you. I know what I'm doing.

LENA. Why didn't we come the short way then?

BOESMAN. Short way? Korsten to Swartkops? What you talking about?

LENA. It didn't use to feel so long. That walk never came to an end. I'm still out there, walking!

BOESMAN. (*A gesture of defeat.*) It's useless to talk to you. (*Goes through* LENA's *bundle and finds two bottles of water. He uncorks one and has a drink. He then starts unpacking his bundle.*)

LENA. All you knew was to load up our things and take the empties back to the bottle store for the deposit. After that . . . ! (*She shakes her head.*) Where we going, Boesman? Don't ask questions. Walk! *Ja,* don't ask questions. Because you didn't know the answers. Where to go, what to do. I remember now. Down this street, up the next one, look down that one, then turn around and go the other way. Not lost? What way takes you past Berry's Corner twice, then back to where you started from? I'm not a fool, Boesman. The roads are crooked enough without you also being lost. First it looked like Redhouse, or Veeplaas. Then it was Bethelsdorp, or maybe Missionvale. Moving along! The dogs want to bite but you can't look down. Look ahead, Sister. To what? Boesman's back. That's the scenery in my world. You don't know what it's like behind you. Look back one day, Boesman. It's me, that thing you drag along the roads. My life. It felt old today. Sitting there on the pavement when you went inside with the empties. Not just tired. It's been that for a long time. Something else. Something that's been used too long. The old pot that leaks, the blanket that can't even keep the fleas warm. Time to throw it away. How do you do that when it's yourself? I was still sore where you hit me. Two white children came and looked while I counted the bruises. There's a big one here, hey. . . . (*Touching a tender spot under one eye.*) You know what I asked them? "Does your mother want a girl? Go ask your mother if she wants a girl." I would have gone, Boesman.

BOESMAN. And then?

LENA. Work for the madam. (BOESMAN *laughs derisively.*) They also laughed and looked some more. *Ja,* look at Lena! Old *Hotnot* bitch. Boesman's her man. Gave her a hiding for dropping the empties. Three bottles broken. Sixpence. Sixpence worth of bruises.

BOESMAN. (*Indifferently.*) You should have gone.

LENA. (*She has to think about it.*) They didn't want me.

BOESMAN. (*Another laugh, then stops himself abruptly.*) You think I want you?

LENA. (*She also thinks about this before answering.*)

You took me. You came out with the wine, put it in your
bundle, then you said "Come!" and walked. I wanted to
say something. The word was in my mouth! But the way
you did it . . . no questions, didn't even look at me . . .
just picked up and walked. So I followed you. Didn't
even know where until I felt the mud between my toes.
Then I knew. Swartkops again! Digging for bait for the
fishermen. Mudprawns and worms in an old jam tin. A
few live ones on top, the dead one at the bottom. "Thirty
cents my *baas*. Just dug them out!" Lie your soul into
hell for enough to live. How we going to dig? We haven't
even got a spade.

BOESMAN. I'll get one.

LENA. Watch out they don't get *you*. Next time they
catch you stealing you're in for keeps! *Haai*, Boesman!
Why here? This place hasn't been good to us. All we've
had next to the river is hard times. (*A little laugh.*) And
wet ones. Remember that night the water came up so
high? When we woke up half drowned with all our things
floating down to the bridge. You got such a fright, you
ran the wrong way. (*She laughs at the memory.*)

BOESMAN. I didn't!

LENA. What were you doing in the deep water? Hav-
ing a wash? (*Another laugh.*) It was almost up with you
that night. Hey! When was that? Last time? (*Pause—
LENA thinks.*) Boesman! When was our last time here?
I'm talking to you. (BOESMAN *deliberately ignores her
and carries on sorting out the contents of his bundle.*)
Boesman!!! (*Pause—no reaction from him.*) Don't be
like that tonight, man. This is a lonely place. Just us two.
Talk to me.

BOESMAN. I've got nothing left to say to you. Talk to
yourself.

LENA. I'll go mad.

BOESMAN. What do you mean "go" mad? You've been
talking to yourself since . . . (*Pause—LENA waits, he
remembers.*) Ja! . . . since our first walk.

LENA. First walk?

BOESMAN. That night, in the brickfields.

LENA. Coega to Veeplaas!

BOESMAN. First you cried. When you stopped crying, you started talking. I was tired. I wanted to sleep. But you talked. "Where we going?" "Let's go back." Who? What? How? Jesus! On and on. Then I thought it. "Boesman, you've made a mistake!"

LENA. Coega to Veeplaas.

BOESMAN. You talked there too. So I thought it again.

LENA. Mistake.

BOESMAN. Mistake. Every time you opened your mouth . . . until I stopped listening.

LENA. I want somebody to listen.

BOESMAN. To what? That *gebabbel* of yours. When you poop it makes more sense. You know why? It stinks. Your words are just noise. Nonsense. The noise of a cursed life. Look at you! Listen to you! You're asking for a lot, Lena. Must I go mad as well?

LENA. I asked you when we came here last. Is that nonsense?

BOESMAN. Yes! What difference does it make? To anything? You're here now!

LENA. (*Looking around.*) I'm here now. (*Surge of anger.*) I know I'm here now. Why? Look at it for God's sake. Is this the best you could do? What was wrong with Veeplaas?

BOESMAN. What's right with it?

LENA. There's other people there! What's the matter with you? Ashamed of yourself? (BOESMAN *turns away from her, dragging their one mattress to the spot where he will build the shelter. He then picks up the piece of corrugated iron and examines it, trying it out in various positions . . . as a roof, a wall, etc.*) Or Missionvale! Redhouse! There's a chance of a job there on the salt-pans. Not even a dog to look at us. Every time we come back here it feels like I've never left. Maybe this is the last time here I'm trying to remember. *Haai!* (*She shakes her head . . . then pauses.*) Wasn't it after Redhouse?

Our last time here. Remember, that farmer chased us off his land. Then we came here. Is that right? (BOESMAN *ignores her.*) Then we went to Korsten.

BOESMAN. After here we went to Korsten?

LENA. *Ja.* (BOESMAN *laughs at her derisively.*) How was it then? (*Pause.*) You won't tell me.

BOESMAN. (*Putting down the piece of iron.*) Make the fire.

LENA. Let's have a *dop* first. I'm feeling the cold. Please, Boesman! (*Without another look at her he walks off.* LENA *gets stiffly to her legs and starts to make the fire. A box is positioned to shield it from the wind, then the bundle of firewood untied, the wood itself broken into pieces, a piece of paper to get it started, etc.*) Walk our legs off for this! Piece of bread and black tea. No butter . . . not even for bruises. (*A thought crosses her mind. She straightens up, thinks hard for a few se·onds then shakes her head.*) No. (*She looks around.*) Maybe he's right. What's the difference? I'm here now. Jesus! After a long life that's a thin slice. No jam on that one. Or Kondens Milk! There's sweetness for you. Maybe if we get lots of prawns . . . (*Another thought. . . . She thinks hard. . . .*) It *was* after Redhouse. Collecting prickly pears. Then they found our place there in the bush. Walk, *Hotnot!* So *Hotnot* walks . . . to Swartkops. Here. The last time here. I was right! (*Pause.*) No, we ran! The farmer had a gun. When he showed us the bullets Boesman dropped his tin and went down that road like a rabbit. . . . (*Laughing . . . her hands to her backside in an imitation of the scene.*) "Don't shoot, baas!" Me too, but the other way. Where did I find him . . . looking at the mud, the hell-in because we had lost all our things again. Just our clothes, and each other. Never lose that. Run your legs off the other way, but at the end of it Boesman is waiting. How the hell does that happen? Redhouse—Swartkops! I was right. He must laugh at himself. (*Back to her chores.*) And then? Somewhere else! *Ja,* of course. One of those other towns.

Veeplaas. Or Missionvale. Maybe Bethelsdorp. Lena
knows them all. (*Pause.*) But which one . . . that time.
(*She straightens up and looks around.*) Which way . . . ?
(*Moving around, trying to orientate herself physically.*)
Let me see now. We came. . . . No. Those lights!
What's that? Where is . . . it's round all right . . .
where the hell is . . . Jesus! I'm right in the middle.
No wonder I get drunk when I try to work it out. . . .
(*Sudden desperation.*) Think, man! It happened to you.
(*Closes her eyes in an effort to remember.*) We were here.
Then we left. Off we go. . . . We're walking . . . and
walking . . . where we walking? Boesman never tells me.
Wait and see. Walking. . . . Somewhere, his shadow. In
front of me. Small man with a long thin shadow. It's
stretching back to me over the veld because we're walk-
ing to the sun and it's going down. . . . Veeplaas! That's
where the sun goes. Behind it there into the bush. So
Veeplaas is . . . (*Looking now for the sun.*) Where the
hell is . . . ? (*Pause.*) Finished. So what? I got it in
here. (*Her head.*)   Redhouse—Swartkops—Veeplaas!
(*She is very pleased with herself.*) Get a move on now.
I'm nearly here. Redhouse—Swartkops—Veeplaas. . . .
(*She carries on working, laying out mugs, filling a little
pot with water, etc. . . . all the time muttering to herself the sequence of places she has established.*) It's coming! Korsten! Empties and the dog. *Hond!* How was it
now? Redhouse—Swartkops—Veeplaas—Korsten. Then
this morning the bulldozers . . . and then . . . (*Pause.*)
Here! I've got there! (*She is very happy.*) Jesus, Sister.
You ran that last bit. Bundle and all. (*She is humming
away happily to herself when* BOESMAN *returns with a
few odds and ends—an old sack, few pieces of wood,
another piece of corrugated iron, an old motorcar door,
etc.—out of which he will fashion their shelter for the
night. He registers* LENA'S *good humour and watches her
suspiciously as he starts to work.* LENA *realizes this and
laughs.*) Why you looking at me so funny? (*He says*

nothing. LENA *hums a little song.*) Remember the times
I used to sing for us? "Da . . . da . . . da. . . ."

BOESMAN. What's the matter with you?

LENA. Feeling fine, darling. I'm warm. You know why?
I've been running. You should have seen me! I'm not as
old as I thought. All the way from Redhouse . . . (*The
rest of her sentence is lost in laughter at the expression
on his face.*) . . . and now I'm here. With you. Da . . .
da . . . da . . .

BOESMAN. (*After watching her for a few more seconds.*) Show me the wine!

LENA. Look for yourself. (BOESMAN *leaves his work on
the shelter. He goes through his bundle and examines two
bottles of wine. They are both intact.* LENA *laughs at
him.*) How's it for a *dop?* (*He puts away the bottles and
goes back to work.*) Hey, you know what I was thinking
just now? A taste of Kondens Milk. What do you say?
If we get lots of prawns. Sugar's not enough, man. I want
some real sweetness. Then you can be as hellish as you
like. (*Starts singing, shuffling out a few dance steps at
the same time.*)

> "A taste of Kondens Milk
> Makes life so sweet.
> Boesman is a Boesman
> Because he's all dark meat."

Look at this! Lena's still got a *vastrap* in her old legs.
You want to dance, Boesman? Not too late to learn. I'll
teach you.

BOESMAN. Just now you get a bloody good *klap!*

LENA. *Ja!* See what I mean. This time I'm laughing,
and you . . . ! Fed-up! You don't like it when somebody
else laughs. Well, you laughed at me for nothing. Because
I was right! Last time here *was* after Redhouse. You
won't mix me up this time. I remember. The farmer
pointed his gun and you were gone, nonstop to Swartkops. Then Veeplaas. Then Korsten. And now here.
How's that! (*Laughs triumphantly.* BOESMAN *lets her
enjoy herself. He waits for his moment.*) And I'm not

finished. Wait and see. I'm going to think some more. I'll work it out, back and back until I reach Coega Kop. Then I'll have it. Coega Kop to here. So what you got to say?

BOESMAN. Nothing.

LENA. (*Another laugh.*) Now you're really the hell-in. Nothing to laugh at.

BOESMAN. Nothing to laugh at? (*He disproves this with a small laugh.*)

LENA. You can't laugh at me. (*Another laugh from* BOESMAN.) I'm right, Boesman!

BOESMAN. How was it? Swartkops after Redhouse?

LENA. Yes!

BOESMAN. And from here we went to . . .

LENA. Korsten! (BOESMAN *shakes his head with another laugh.*) It's no good, Boesman. I know what you're trying. You're not going to do it this time. Go laugh at yourself. (*Goes back to her work, but there is an edge of something now in her voice as she repeats the sequence with exaggerated emphasis.*) Redhouse—Swartkops—Veeplaas—Korsten . . . here! Where I am. (*Looks up at* BOESMAN, *but he pretends total indifference. This adds to her growing uncertainty. She looks around . . . we see her trying hard to remember, to work it out yet again.* BOESMAN *waits. He knows. Eventually . . .*) Is it wrong?

BOESMAN. (*Strolling up to the fire to fetch something.*) Why do you stop singing?

LENA. Is it wrong, Boesman?

BOESMAN. (*He takes his time, finding whatever he is looking for first before answering.*) What about . . . Swartkops—Veeplaas—Redhouse?

LENA. (*Vacantly.*) Swartkops . . . Veeplaas . . .

BOESMAN. Or this. Veeplaas.

LENA. Veeplaas.

BOESMAN. Redhouse . . .

LENA. Redhouse . . .

BOESMAN. Korsten!

LENA. Veeplaas — Redhouse — Korsten? (*Pause.*) Where's Swartkops? (*The sight of her vacant confusion is too much for* BOESMAN. *He has a good laugh, now thoroughly enjoying himself.*) To hell with it! I'm not listening to you. I'm here!

BOESMAN. Where? Veeplaas?

LENA. (*Closing her eyes.*) I'm here. I know how I got here. Redhouse, then Swartkops . . . (*Pause—she has forgotten.*) Wait . . . ! Redhouse—Swartkops . . .

BOESMAN. Go on! But don't forget Bethelsdorp this time. You've been there too. And Missionvale. And Kleinskool.

LENA. Don't mix me up, Boesman! (*Trying desperately to remember her sequence.*) Redhouse—Swartkops . . . then Veeplaas . . . then . . .

BOESMAN. It's wrong! (*Pause . . . she looks at him desperately. He leaves his work on the shelter and goes to her.*) Yes! It's wrong! Now what you going to do?

LENA. (*Moves around helplessly, trying to orientate herself physically.*) It's mixed up again. I had it!

BOESMAN. Look at you! *Babalas!* . . . from yesterday's wine. Yesterday you were drunk, today you're hung-over. One or the other. Your whole life.

LENA. (*Staring off in a direction.*) Over there . . . Where did the sun go . . . ?

BOESMAN. (*Joining her.*) What you looking for?

LENA. Veeplaas.

BOESMAN. That way? (LENA *studies* BOESMAN's *face for a second, then decides she is wrong.*)

LENA. No. (*Moving in a different direction.*) That way!

BOESMAN. Wrong! (LENA *tries yet another direction.*) Wrong! Jesus, Lena! You're lost.

LENA. Do you really know, Boesman? Where and how . . .

BOESMAN. Yes!

LENA. Tell me. (*He laughs.*) Help me, Boesman!

BOESMAN. What? Find yourself? (BOESMAN *launches*

into a grotesque pantomime of a search. LENA *watches him with hatred. Calling:*) Lena! Lena! (*He rejoins her.*) Sorry, Auntie. Better go to Veeplaas. Maybe you're there.

LENA. (*Directly at* BOESMAN, *her anger overwhelming her.*) You low bastard. Pig! Yes, you. You're a pig. It's a sin, Boesman. (*He enjoys her tirade immensely.*) Wait a bit! One day . . . !

BOESMAN. One day what?

LENA. Something's going to happen.

BOESMAN. That's right.

LENA. What?

BOESMAN. Something's going to happen.

LENA. *Ja!* (*Pause.*) What's going to happen?

BOESMAN. I thought you knew. One day you'll ask me who you are. (*He laughs.*)

LENA. *Ja,* another good laugh for you that day.

BOESMAN. The best one! "*Ek se ou pêllie* . . . who am I?" (*More laughter.*)

LENA. (*Trying her name.*) Lena . . . Lena . . .

BOESMAN. What about Rosie? Nice name Rose. Maria. Anna. Or Sannie! Sannie who? *Sommer* Sannie Somebody.

LENA. NO!

BOESMAN. (*Ready to laugh.*) Who are you?

LENA. Mary. I want to be Mary. Who are you? (*The laugh dies on* BOESMAN's *lips.*) That's what I ask next. *Ja,* you! Who's this man? And then I'm gone. Goodbye, darling. I've had enough. S'truesgod, that day I'm gone.

BOESMAN. You mean that day you get a bloody *good* hiding.

LENA. *Aikona!* I'll go to the police.

BOESMAN. You tried that before and what happened? "She's my woman, *baas.* Just warmed her up a little bit." "Take her" . . . finish *en klaar.* They know the way it is with our sort.

LENA. Not this time! My name is Mary, remember. "Don't know this man, *baas.*" So where's your proof?

BOESMAN. (*Holding up a clenched fist.*) Here!

LENA. Watch out! You'll get too far one day. Death penalty.

BOESMAN. For you? (*Derisive laughter.*) Not guilty and discharge.

LENA. Don't talk big. You're frightened of the rope. When you stop hitting it's not because you're tired or had enough. You're frightened! *Ja.* (*Pause.*) *Ja.* That's when I feel it most. When you do it carefully. The last few . . . when you aim. I count them. One . . . another one . . . wait for the next one! He's only resting. (*Pause.*) You're right, Boesman. That's proof. When I feel it I'll know. I'm Lena.

BOESMAN. (*Emphatically.*) And I'm Boesman.

LENA. Boesman and Lena.

BOESMAN. Yes! That's who. That's what. When . . . where . . . why! All your bloody nonsense questions. That's the answer.

LENA. Boesman and Lena.

BOESMAN. So stop asking them! (*Pause . . . he goes back to work on the shelter. He tries the "answer" for himself.*) Boesman and Lena. *Ja!* It explains. So it's another rotten hole for the rotten people, eh? Look at it! Useless, hey? If it rains tonight you'll get wet. If it blows hard you'll be counting stars.

LENA. I know what it's like in there!

BOESMAN. It's all you'll ever know.

LENA. I'm sick of it.

BOESMAN. Sick of it! You want to live in a house? What do you think you are? A white madam?

LENA. It wasn't always like this. There were better times.

BOESMAN. In your dreams maybe.

LENA. What about Veeplaas? Chopping wood for the Chinaman? That room in his backyard. Real room, with a door and all that.

BOESMAN. Forget it. *Now* is the only time in your life.

LENA. No! Now. What's that? I wasn't born today. I want my life. Where's it?

BOESMAN. In the mud, where you are. *Now.* Tomorrow it will be there too, and the next day. And if you're still alive when I've had enough of this, you'll load up and walk, somewhere else.

LENA. Roll up in my blanket and crawl into that! (*The shelter.*) Never enough wine to make us sleep the whole night. Wake up in the dark. The fire cold. What time is that in my life? Another now! Black now and empty as hell. Even when you're also awake. You make it worse. When I call you, and I know you hear me, but you say nothing. Sometimes loneliness is two . . . you and the other person who doesn't want to know you're there. I'm sick of you too, Boesman!

BOESMAN. So go.

LENA. Don't joke. I'll walk tonight. I will.

BOESMAN. Go! Goodbye, darling. (LENA *takes a few steps away from the fire, then stops.* BOESMAN *watches her.*) You still lost? Okay. Boesman will help you tonight. That way is Veeplaas. Through Swartkops, over the railway line, past that big thing with chimneys. Then you come to the veld. There's a path. Walk it until you see little lights. That's Veeplaas. Redhouse is that way. Korsten is over there. What else you want? Bethelsdorp? Coega Kop? There! There! I know my way. I know my world. (LENA *is standing still.*) So what you waiting for? Walk!

LENA. (*Her back to him, staring into the darkness.*) There's somebody out there. (*Pause.* BOESMAN *leaves his work on the shanty and joins her. They stare in silence for a few seconds.*)

BOESMAN. Drunk.

LENA. No.

BOESMAN. Look at him!

LENA. (*Shaking her head.*) Nobody comes to the mud flats to get drunk.

BOESMAN. What do you know?

LENA. He's stopped. Maybe he's going to dig.

BOESMAN. Dark before the water's low.

LENA. Or a whiteman.

BOESMAN. When did you see a whiteman sitting like that!?

LENA. Maybe he sees us. (*She waves.*)

BOESMAN. (*Stopping her.*) What's the matter with you?

LENA. Go see what he wants.

BOESMAN. And then?

LENA. Do something. Help him.

BOESMAN. We got no help.

LENA. I'm not thinking of him. (BOESMAN *stares at her.*) It's another person, Boesman.

BOESMAN. I'm warning you! Don't start any nonsense. (*Moves back to the shelter.* LENA *watches him for a few seconds, then decides.*)

LENA. (*Calling to the other person.*) Hey, I say.

BOESMAN. Lena!

LENA. (*Ignoring* BOESMAN.) We got a fire!

BOESMAN. Lena!

LENA. Come over!

BOESMAN. You damned . . .

LENA. (*Sees the violence coming and moves away quickly.*) To hell with you! I want him. (*Calling.*) Hey, darling! Come this way! (*To* BOESMAN.) Sit in the dark and talk to myself because you don't hear me anymore? No, Boesman! I want him! Hey! He's coming. (*A moment of mutual uncertainty at the approach of the stranger.* LENA *falls back to* BOESMAN'S *side. He picks up a stick in readiness for trouble. They stand together, waiting. An old African appears slowly. Hat on his head, the rest of him is lost in the folds of a shabby old overcoat. He is an image of age and decrepitude.*)

BOESMAN. A Kaffir!

LENA. An old Kaffir! (LENA *almost turns away with disappointment.* BOESMAN *sees this and has a good laugh.*)

BOESMAN. Lena calls out in the dark, and what does she get? Look at it.

LENA. (*After a few more seconds of hesitation.*) Better than nothing.

BOESMAN. So? Go on. You wanted somebody. There's a black one. (LENA *takes a few steps towards the old man. He has remained at a distance. As* LENA *approaches him he murmurs a greeting in Xhosa.*)

OLD AFRICAN. *Molweni.* (Good evening.)

LENA. *Molo Outa.* (BOESMAN *watches this and* LENA'S *other attempts to communicate with the old man, with cruel amusement. She gets another murmur from the old man.*)

OLD AFRICAN. *N'njani. Nisaphila. Vukani.* (How are you? How do you do?)

BOESMAN. What you waiting for?

LENA. I am Lena. This is my man Boesman.

BOESMAN. Shake his hand! Fancy *Hotnot* like you. Give him some smart stuff. "How do you do, darling." (*The old man murmurs something in Xhosa.*)

OLD AFRICAN. *Ngi Wabatutu. Onasha. Ngi lahlegile. Ngi funana nehlobo zami. Ngi hamba kudala. Inyayo zami zikhathele.* (I am Wabatutu. Onasha tribe. I'm lost. I have been looking for my relatives. I have been walking for a long time. My legs are tired.)

LENA. What's that? You know his language. (BOES-MAN *laughs.*) Does the *Outa* want something?

OLD AFRICAN. *Ngethe ngi funana nehlobo zami. Ngi lahlegile. Ngi lahlegile. Inyayo zami zikhathele—zikhathele!* (I said that I'm looking for my relatives. I'm lost. I'm lost. My legs are tired—tired!)

LENA. Don't you speak English or Afrikaans? *"Môre Baas!"*

BOESMAN. Give him some help.

LENA. He doesn't look so good. (*A few steps closer to the old man.*) Come sit, *Outa.* Sit and rest. (*Nothing happens. She turns to* BOESMAN.) How do you say that in the Kaffir tongue?

BOESMAN. *Hamba.*

LENA. Alright, Boesman! (*Back to the old man—she*

pushes forward a box.) It's warm by the fire. (*Nothing happens . . . a spark of anger in her voice.*) You deaf? Sit! (*The old man does so.*) Ja, rest your legs. They work hard for us poor people. (BOESMAN *looks up in time to see her uncorking one of their bottles of water. They stare at each other in silence for a few seconds.*) Maybe he's thirsty.

BOESMAN. And us?

LENA. Only water.

BOESMAN. It's scarce here.

LENA. I'll fetch from Swartkops tomorrow.

BOESMAN. To hell! He doesn't belong to us. (*Grabs the bottle away from her and together with the other one puts it inside the shanty.*)

LENA. There was plenty of times his sort gave us water on the road.

BOESMAN. It's different now.

LENA. How?

BOESMAN. Because I say so.

LENA. Because this time you got the water, hey! (*Back to the old man.*) Does *Outa* come far? (*She stands and waits . . . nothing.*) We're from Korsten. They kicked us out there this morning. (*Nothing.*) It's a hard life for us brown people, hey?

BOESMAN. He's not brown people, he's black people.

LENA. They got feelings too. Not so, *Outa?*

BOESMAN. You'll get some feelings if you don't watch that fire. (LENA *is waiting for a word from the old man with growing desperation and irritation.*)

LENA. What's the matter? You sick? Where's it hurt? (*Nothing.*) Hey! I'm speaking to you. (*The old man murmurs in Xhosa.*)

OLD AFRICAN. *Singibongile. Ngi bonga. Hau mtwanami, ngethe guwe, ngi Wabatutu. Ngi hamba kudala funana nehlobo zami. Mini yonke, ubusuku bonke. Ngi lahlegile. Ngi khathele!* (Thank you for your hospitality. I thank you very much. My child, I said to you, I am Wabatutu.

I have been walking for a long time looking for my relatives. All day, all night. I'm lost. I'm tired!)

LENA. Stop that baboon language! Where's it sore? (*Another unintelligible response.* LENA *turns away in violent disgust.*) *Ag*, go to hell! Stupid Kaffir. Jawed my bloody head off for nothing! (BOESMAN *explodes into laughter at this ending to* LENA's *encounter with the old man.*)

BOESMAN. Finished with him already? Oh, no, man! You must try something there. He's so much better than nothing. Or was nothing better? Too bad you're both so useless. Could have worked a point. Some sports. You and him. They like *Hotnot* bitches. Black bastards! (LENA *is wandering around helplessly.*) Going to call again? You'll end up with a tribe of old Kaffirs sitting here. That's all you'll get out of that darkness. They go there to die. I'm warning you, Lena! Pull another one in here and you'll do the rest of your talking tonight with a thick mouth. Turn my place into a Kaffir nest!

LENA. (*Coming back dejectedly to the fire.*) Give me a drink, Boesman.

BOESMAN. That's better. Now you're talking like a *Hotnot*. Away world, come brandywine!

LENA. A drink, please, man!

BOESMAN. You look like one too now. A real one. Ass on the ground, crying for a bottle.

LENA. (*Really desperate.*) Then open one.

BOESMAN. All that fancy talk is thirsty work, hey?

LENA. Open a bottle, Boesman!

BOESMAN. When I'm ready.

LENA. (*She stands.*) One of them is mine! (*Waits for a reaction from* BOESMAN, *but gets none.*) I want it now! (*Pause.*) I'm going to take it, Boesman. (*Moves forward impulsively to where the bottles are hidden.* BOESMAN *lets her take a few steps, then goes into action.*)

BOESMAN. (*Grabbing a stick.*) Okay!

LENA. (*Seeing it coming.*) *Eina!* (*Running quickly to*

the old man.) Watch now, *Outa.* You be witness for me.
Watch! He's going to kill me.

BOESMAN. (*Stopping.*) You asking for it tonight, Lena.

LENA. You see how it is, *Outa?*

BOESMAN. He'll see you get it if you don't watch out.

LENA. I got it this morning!

BOESMAN. Just touch those bottles and you'll get it
again. (*Throws down the stick and goes off.*)

LENA. (*Shouting after him.*) Go on! Why don't you
hit me? There's no white *baases* here to laugh. Does this
old thing worry you? (*Turning back to the old man.*)
Look, *Outa.* I want you to look. (*Showing him the bruises
on her arms and fare.*) No, not that one. That's an old
one. This one. And here. Just because I dropped the sack
with the empties. I would have been dead if they hadn't
laughed. When other people laugh he gets ashamed. Now
too. I would have got it hard from him if you . . .
(*Pause.*) Why didn't you laugh? They laughed this
morning. They laugh every time. (*Growing violence.*)
What's the matter with you? Kaffirs laugh at it too. It's
really funny. Me! Old bitch being clobbered! (*Pause—
she moves away to some small chore at the fire. After
this she looks up at the old man, and then goes back
slowly to him.*) Wasn't it funny? (*She moves closer.*)
Hey, look at me! (*He looks at her.*) My name is Lena.
(*She pats herself on the chest. Nothing happens. She
tries again, but this time she pats him.*) Outa . . . You
. . . (*Patting herself.*) . . . Lena . . . me.

OLD AFRICAN. Lena.

LENA. (*Excited.*) *Ewe!* Lena!

OLD AFRICAN. Lena.

LENA. (*Softly.*) "My God!" (*Looks around desperately, then after a quick look in the direction in which
BOESMAN disappeared she goes to the half-finished shelter
and fetches one of the bottles of water. She uncorks it
and hurries back to the old man. Offering the bottle.*)
Water. *Water!* (Afrikaans.) *Manzi!* (*Helps him get it to
his lips. He drinks. In between mouthfuls he murmurs*

away in Xhosa. LENA *picks up odd phrases and echoes them, as if she understood him. The whole of his monologue follows this pattern: the old man murmuring intermittently—the occasional phrase or even sentence quite clear—and* LENA *surrendering herself more and more to the illusion of conversation.*)

OLD AFRICAN. *Singibongile. Mamela mtwanami. Ngethe guwe, ngi funana nehlobo zami. Ngi lahlegile! Ngi vela e Bayi. Ngi bege e Tenage. Ngi hamba kudala. Mini yonke, ubusuku bonke. Ngi uthatha. Inyayo zami zikhathele. Safa . . . safa.* (Thank you for your hospitality. Listen, child. I said to you, I am looking for my relatives. I'm lost! I am from Port Elizabeth. I am going to Tenage. I have been walking for a long time. All day long, all night long. I'm an old man. My legs are tired. Hard times . . . hard times.)

LENA. (*Intermittently echoes phrases of the* OLD AFRICAN'S *speech, ending with:*) *Safa . . . safa.* What's all that mean? (*He hands her back the bottle.*) If *Outa's* saying . . . (*Stops, takes another quick look to make sure* BOESMAN *is out of sight, then returns to the old man's side. She speaks secretively and with intensity.*) It's true! You're right. (*He is still murmuring.*)

OLD AFRICAN. *Ngethe guwe ngi lahlegile! Lahlegile! Qonda? Qonda? Mamela hau mtwanami. Ngi vela e Bayi. Ngi bege e Tenage. Ngi funana nehlobo zami. Ngi hamba intabane, etjanini e hlathini. Ubusuku bonke, mini yonke, ngi hamba, ngi funana. Ngi hamba, ngi funana. Ngi lahlegile! Inyayo zami zikhathele. Qonda? Ngo zikhathele. Ngi lahlegile. Ngi lahlegile!* (I said to you I am lost! Lost! Understand? Understand? Listen, my child. I am from Port Elizabeth. I am going to Tenage. I have been looking for my relatives. I have traveled across the mountains, plains and through the forest. All night long, all day long, I've been walking, I've been looking. (*Repeats.*) I've been walking, I've been looking. I'm lost! My legs are tired. Understand? I'm tired. I'm lost. I'm lost!)

LENA. Wait now. Listen to mine. I had a dog. In Korsten. Just a mongrel. Once when we were sitting somewhere counting our bottles and eating he came and looked at us. Must have been a Kaffir *hond*. He didn't bark. I left some bread for him there on the ground when we went. He ate it and followed us all the way back to Korsten. (*Another look over her shoulder to make sure* BOESMAN *isn't near. She continues her story in an even lower tone.*) For two days like that around our place there. When Boesman wasn't looking I threw him things to eat. Boesman knew I was up to something. I'm a bloody fool, *Outa*. Something makes me happy I start singing. So every time Boesman saw the dog, he throws stones. He doesn't like dogs. They don't like him. But when he wasn't looking I threw food. (*Laughs secretively.*) I won, *Outa!* One night the dog came in when he was asleep . . . came and sat and looked at me. When Boesman woke up, he moved out. So it was every night after that. We waited for Boesman to sleep, then he came and watched me. All the things I did—making the fire, cooking, counting bottles or bruises, even just sitting, you know, when it's too much . . . he saw it. Dog! I called him Dog. But any name, he'd wag his tail if you said it nice. I'll tell you what it is. Eyes, *Outa*. Another pair of eyes. Something to see you. Then this morning in all the *lawaai* and mix-up—gone! I wanted to look, but Boesman was in a hurry. So what! Now I got *Outa*. (*Nudging him.*) Lena!

OLD AFRICAN. Lena.

LENA. (*Little laugh.*) You see, I'm not ashamed. DE! (*In a fit of generosity she passes the bottle over again.*) Much as you like, darling. Doesn't cost a penny. Drink. Don't worry about him. He's worried about the wine. (*Old man drinks.*) No heart in that one, *Outa*. Or empty. Dried-up. Two-penny deposit for Boseman's heart, like a brandy bottle, but empty. (*Gets the bottle back and takes it to the shelter, talking all the time.*) *Outa* know the empties. Brandy bottles, beer bottles, wine bottles.

Any kind. Medicine. Tomato sauce. Sell them at the Bottle Exchange. We were doing good with the empties there in Korsten. Whiteman's drinking himself to death. Take your sack, knock on some back doors and it's full by no time. It was going easy for us, man. Eating meat. Proper chops! Then this morning: Walk, *Hotnot!* Just had time to grab our things. That's when I dropped the sack. Three bottles broken. I didn't even have on pants or a petticoat when we started walking. (*Straightens up at the shelter and registers the old man sitting quietly.*) You're a nice old . . . (*Correcting herself.*) . . . you're one of the good *Bantus,* hey? I can see it. Sit so nice and listen to Lena. (*Back to the fire where she puts on a few more pieces of wood.*) That's why we called. I could see it. I said to Boesman: "He's one of the good ones. Poor old thing!" Sorry feelings—for you. "Let's call him over!" (*Old man starts murmuring again. This time it is accompanied by much head shaking.* LENA *interprets this as a rejection of what she has just said.*)

OLD AFRICAN. *Mamela mtwanami. Ngi funa uku hamba. Singibongile. Angina e sekhathi. Ngi qonde. Ngi qonde . . . qonde!* (Listen, my child. I'm leaving. Thank you for your hospitality. I have no time left. I'm going. I'm going . . . going!)

LENA. No, *Outa,* I did! *Haai,* it's true! Why should I lie? (*Her tone and manner become progressively more angry.*) It's true! What do you know? Don't argue! Bloody old . . . (*The old man makes a move to stand up.* LENA, *changing tone and attitude, forces him to stay seated.*) Okay! Okay! Okay, *Outa!!* I'll tell you the truth. But mustn't say I lie. Sit still. (*Pause.*) It's my eyes. They're not so good anymore, specially when the thing is far away. But in the old days . . . ! You know those mountains out there, when you walk Kleinskool way . . . ? In the old days so clear, *Outa.* When we were resting I used to put my finger on a point, and then up and down, just the way it is. (*Demonstrates tracing the outline of a mountain range.*) I haven't seen them for a long time. Boesman's back gets in the way these days. (*Breaking mood.*) It's not so bad, when the thing is near to me. Like Korsten, this morning. That's quite clear. Tomorrow as well. I can see that too, we'll be digging. I say! Old Lena's talking her head off tonight. And you sit so nicely and listen to her. Boesman wouldn't. Tell me to shut up. (*Secretively.*) We must be careful. He'll try and chase you away just now. Mustn't go, you see. (*The old man starts murmuring again. For a few seconds* LENA *interprets it as "small talk" as she goes on preparing for their supper.*)

OLD AFRICAN. *Mamela hau mtwanami. Ngi uthatha. Qonda? E zhesha lemkile. Sesifikile. Sesifikile! Ngi hamba kampeni. Ngethe guwe, ngi Wabatutu. Ngi vela e Bayi. Ngi bege e Tenage. Ngi lahlegile. Lahlegile! Ngi funana nehlobo zami e Tenage. Ngi funana kudala. Intabane, etjanini e hlathini. Mini yonke inyoka hamba etjanini. Ubusuku bonke nga bona umhlold. Ne senja zinkongkothe. Zinkongkothe, zinkongkothe!* (Listen, my child. I am an old man. Understand? I have little time left. I'm dying. I'm dying! I walk into your camp. I said to you, I am Wabatutu. I am from Port Elizabeth. I am going to Tenage. I'm lost. Lost! I'm looking for my relatives at Tenage. I've been looking for a long time. Mountains, plains and forests. All day long buzzards follow me across the plains. At night I saw strange things. Dogs barking. Barking, barking!)

LENA. That's right. Of course. *Ja*, it's going to be cold tonight. You never said a truer thing, darling. I know, I know. Don't you worry. We'll eat just now. Won't take long to boil. (*Pause—the old man mumbles away.* LENA *studies him in silence for a few seconds.*)

OLD AFRICAN. *Inkosazana e ntle. Indoda yaku ayingithande. Ngi uthlolo ingathazeko ni. Qonda? Indoda umfana ayingithande, ngoba ngi uthatha. Qonda?* (You are a very nice woman. Your husband does not like me. I am sorry for the trouble I have caused you. Understand?

Your husband is a young man and doesn't like me, because I am an old man. Understand?)

LENA. (*Interrupting him.*) It's about Boesman, isn't it? (*Laughs.*) I really understand. Why shouldn't you and me talk? Well . . . Too small for a real *Hotnot*, *Outa*. There's something else there. Bushman blood. And wild! That two-penny deposit heart of his is tight, like his poophole and his fist. (*Holds up a clenched fist in an imitation of* BOESMAN.) That's how he talks to the world. (*Much laughter from* LENA *at her joke, with a lot of nudging and back slapping as if the old man was also laughing. He isn't.*) *Ja,* so it goes. He walks in front. I walk behind. It used to be side by side, with jokes. At night he let me sing, and listened. Never learnt any songs himself. (*The old man murmurs.*)

OLD AFRICAN. *Mamela Mtwanami. Ngethe guwe, indoda yaku ayingithande. Ngi uthatha. Indoda yaku umfana. Sesifikile. Sesifikile! Angina e sekhathi. Sesifikile!* (Listen, child. I said to you, your husband does not like me. Your husband is a young man. I am dying. I'm dying! I have no time left. I'm dying!)

LENA. I don't know. (*Old man continues to murmur,* LENA *gets desperate.*) Don't start again, *Outa.* I don't know! Behind us. Isn't that enough? Too heavy to carry. The last time we joked, the last time I sang. Behind us somewhere. Our rubbish. We'll leave something here too if there's any last times left. Jesus! It's so heavy now, *Outa.* Am I crooked? It feels that way when we stop and the bundles come down. What's so heavy? I walk and I think . . . a blanket, a few things in a bucket. . . . Look! (*Their possessions.*) And even when they're down, when you've made your place and the fire is burning and you rest your legs, something stays heavy. Hey! Once you've put your life on your head and walked you never get light again. We've been walking a long time, *Outa.* Look at my feet. Those little paths on the *veld* . . . Boesman and Lena helped write them. I meet the memory of myself on the old roads. Sometimes young.

Sometimes old. Is she coming or going? From where to where? All mixed-up. The right time on the wrong road, the right road leading to the wrong place. (*Murmur from the old man.*)

OLD AFRICAN. *Umlilo, inje shiza. Ngi hamba kudala. Singibongile. Ngi uthlolo ingathazeko ni. Godwa ngi senhleleni. Ngethe guwe, ngi funana nehlobo zami. Angina e sekhathi. Sesifikile. Sesifikile.* (The fire, it is warm. I have been walking for a long time. Thank you for your hospitality. I'm sorry for the trouble I have caused you. But I must leave. I said to you, I am looking for my relatives. I have no time left. I'm dying. I'm dying!)

LENA. He won't tell me. That's a sin, isn't it? He'll be punished. But he says there's no God for us. Do you know? Up there! (*A vague gesture to the sky. No intelligible response from the old man.*) Doesn't matter. (*Old man murmurs loudly, urgently.*) What's that now? Maybe . . . (*Straightening up at the fire.*) Jesus, *Outa!* You're asking things tonight. (*Sharply.*) Why do you want to know? (*Pause.*) It's a long story. (*Moves over to him, sits down beside him.*) One, *Outa*, that lived. For six months. The others were born dead. (*Pause.*)

OLD AFRICAN. *Hau mtwanami. Uwkhumbuza u Tasha, hau mtwanami. Nhethe guwe, umlilo, inje shiza. Singibongile. Ngi hamba kudala. Inyayo zami zikhathele. Godwa ngi senhleleni. Ngi funana nehlolo zami. Mini yonke, ubusuku bonke. Nga bona umhlold. Ngi hamba, hamba, hamba! Inyayo zami zikhathele. Ne senja zinkongkothe, zinkongkothe. Ubusuku bonke. Zinkongkothe, zinkongkothe, zinkongkothe . . .* (My child. You remind me of Tasha, my daughter. I said to you, the fire, it is warm. Thank you for your hospitality. I have been walking for a long time. My legs are tired. But I must leave. I have been looking for my relatives. All day, all night. I saw strange things. I have run, run, run! My legs are tired. The dogs barking, barking. All night long. Barking, barking, barking. . . .)

LENA. That all? *Ja.* Only a few words I know, but a long story if you lived it. (*Murmuring from the old man.*) That's all. That's all. Jesus God, *Outa!* What more must I say? What you asking me about? Pain? Yes! Don't *Kaffirs* know what that means? One night it was longer than a small piece of candle and then as big as darkness. Somewhere else a donkey looked at it. I crawled under the cart and they looked. Boesman was too far away to call. Just the sound of his axe as he chopped wood. I didn't even have rags! You asked me and now I've told you. Pain is a candle-stump and a donkey's face. What's that mean to you? You weren't there. Nobody was. Why do you ask *now?* You're too late for that. *This* is what I feel now . . . (*The fire, the shelter, her "here and now."*) . . . This! My life is here tonight. Tomorrow or the next day that one out there will drag it somewhere else. But tonight I sit *here.* You interested in that? (*The old man gets slowly to his feet and starts to move away.* LENA *throws herself at him violently.*)

OLD AFRICAN. *Mamela hau mtwanami. Ngi funa uku hamba! Angina e sekhathi. Singibongile. Ngi funa uku hamba* . . . (Listen, my child. I am leaving! I have no time left. Thank you for your hospitality. I am leaving. . . .)

LENA. Not a damn! I'm not finished! You can't just go, walk away like you didn't hear. You asked me, and I've told you. This is what I'm left with. You've got two eyes. Sit and look! (*She has forced the old man back on to his box.* LENA *calms down.*) Lena!

OLD AFRICAN. Lena.

LENA. (*Trying to mollify him.*) I'll ask Boesman to give you a *dop.* Okay? Won't be too bad. Where could you go now? Dark out there, *Outa.* Something will grab you. (*Hears a noise—moves away a few steps and peers into the darkness.*) He's coming. Listen, we must be clever now. Don't look happy. And don't say anything. Just sit still. Pretend we still don't like each other. (*Back to her fire. Another idea sends her back hurriedly to the*

old man.) No. I know what you do. When he comes back
you must say you'll buy wine for us all tomorrow. Say
you got a job in Swartkops and when you get your pay
you'll buy wine. You hear me? (*Violently.*) Hey . . . !
(*Before she can say anything more* BOESMAN *appears.
He has a few more pieces of firewood, and something else
for the shelter.* LENA *scuttles back to the fire, and makes
herself busy.* BOESMAN *stops and stares at the two of
them.*)

BOESMAN. What you been doing?

LENA. (*Innocently.*) Nothing. Look at the wine if you
don't believe me.

BOESMAN. Then why's he still here?

LENA. I been looking after the fire. Water's nearly
boiling.

BOESMAN. *You* called him . . . *you* tell him to go.

LENA. (*Looking furtively at the old man, waiting for
him to speak.*) This wood doesn't mean much. Won't last
the night.

BOESMAN. Don't pretend you didn't hear.

LENA. Okay. (*Tries to lose herself in fussing with the
pot.* BOESMAN *waits.*)

BOESMAN. So when you going to tell him to go?

LENA. Who?

BOESMAN. Don't play stupid with me, Lena!

LENA. Him? Slowly there. (*Leaves the fire and talks
to him with an exaggerated show of secrecy.*) He's okay.

BOESMAN. What's that mean?

LENA. Good *Kaffir.*

BOESMAN. How do you know?

LENA. (*To the old man.*) Tell him what you said to
me, *Outa.*

BOESMAN. Since when can you speak his language?

LENA. He's got a few words of Afrikaans. *Outa!!*

BOESMAN. What did he say?

LENA. He said he's going to buy wine tomorrow. (*To
the old man.*) Not so? He's got some jobs there in
Swartkops. Some garden jobs. Ask him.

BOESMAN. Who's going to give *that* a job?

LENA. Somebody with a soft heart.

BOESMAN. You mean a soft head.

LENA. (*Forcing a laugh.*) Soft head! Bloody good, Boesman.

BOESMAN. Garden job! He hasn't got enough left in him to dig his own grave.

LENA. Soft heart and a soft head! *Haai!* (LENA *is laughing too much.* BOESMAN *stares at her. She stops, weakly.*) Funny little joke.

(BOESMAN'S *suspicions are aroused. He goes back to work on the shelter, but watches the other two very carefully.* LENA, *thinking she has won, starts to lay out their supper.*)

LENA. (*Loaf of brown bread.*) Can I break it in three pieces?

BOESMAN. Two pieces! (LENA *wants to rebuke him, but stops herself in time.*)

LENA. (*Softly to the old man.*) We'll share mine. (*Looks up to see* BOESMAN *watching her.*) *Pondokkie's* looking okay. Clever little nest. He's good with his hands, *Outa.* (*Without realizing what she is doing,* LENA *starts humming a little song as she works away at the fire. She realizes her mistake too late.* BOESMAN *is staring hard at her when she looks up. Desperately:*) I'm not happy!

BOESMAN. You're up to something.

LENA. S'truesgod I'm not happy.

BOESMAN. He must go.

LENA. Please, Boesman!

BOESMAN. He's had his rest. Hey!

LENA. It's dark now.

BOESMAN. That's his troubles. Hey! *Hamba Wena.*

LENA. He's not doing any harm.

BOESMAN. He'll bring the others. It's not far to their location from here.

LENA. Boesman! Just for once a favor. Let him stay.

BOESMAN. What's he to me?

LENA. For me, man. (*Pause.*) I want him.

BOESMAN. What for? What you up to, Lena? (*Pause—*
LENA *can't answer his questions.*)

LENA. (*Impulsively.*) You can have the wine. All of it.
Next time as well. (*Dives to the shelter, produces the two
bottles of wine.*) There!

BOESMAN. (*Unbelievingly.*) For that!

LENA. I want him.

BOESMAN. This is wine, Lena. That's a Kaffir. He
won't help you forget. You want to sit sober in this
world? You know what it looks like then?

LENA. I want him.

BOESMAN. (*Shaking his head.*) You off your mind tonight. (*To the old man.*) You're an expensive old turd.
Two bottles of wine! *Ek sê.* Boesman has party tonight.
(*He tantalizes* LENA *by opening a bottle and passing it
under her nose.*) Smell! *Hotnot's* forget-me-not. (*First
mouthful.*) Away world, come brandywine!

LENA. (*Restraining the old man.*) No, *Outa.* I've paid.
You can stay the night with us. If we all lie together it
will be warm in there.

BOESMAN. (*Overhearing.*) What do you mean?

LENA. (*After a pause.*) You can have the mattress.

BOESMAN. To hell! He's not coming inside. Bring your
Kaffir and his fleas into my *pondok?* Not a damn.

LENA. He won't sit there by himself.

BOESMAN. Then sit with him! (*He sees* LENA's *di-
lemma . . . enjoys it.*) *Ja!* You can choose. Inside here
or take your fleas and keep him company. (*Pause.* BOES-
MAN *works away, tries to whistle.*) I said you can sleep
inside with me or . . .

LENA. I heard you, Boesman.

BOESMAN. So? (LENA *doesn't answer.* BOESMAN *rubs it
in.*) It's going to be cold tonight. When it starts pushing
and the water comes back. Boesman's all right. Two
bottles and a pondokkie. Ass-high! (*Watches* LENA. *She
moves slowly to their things. For the first time he is un-*

sure of himself.) What you going to do? (LENA *doesn't answer. She finds one of their blankets and takes it to the old man.*)

LENA. Here, *Outa.* We'll need it.

BOESMAN. (*Suddenly on his feet.*) I've changed my mind. He must go.

LENA. (*Turning on him with unexpected ferocity.*) Be careful, Boesman!

BOESMAN. Of what?

LENA. (*Eyes closed, fists clenched.*) Be careful. (*Her tone stops him. He sits down again, now even more unsure of himself.*)

BOESMAN. You think I care what you do? You want to sit outside and die of cold with a Kaffir, go ahead!

LENA. I'd sit out there with a dog tonight! (*Turns back to the old man.*) We'll need more wood. And something in case it rains. I'm not so handy at making shelter, *Outa.* (*To* BOESMAN.) Where did you find that stuff? Anything left out there? (*This time* BOESMAN *doesn't answer. He stares at her with hard disbelief.*) I'll see what I can find, *Outa.* (*Wanders off.* BOESMAN, *in front of his shelter with the two bottles of wine, watches her go. When she has disappeared he studies the old man. Takes a few more swallows, then gets up and moves a few steps in the direction that* LENA *left. Certain that she is not about, he turns and goes back to the old man.*)

BOESMAN. (*Standing over him.*) Hond! (*The old man looks up at him.* BOESMAN *pulls the blanket away from him.*) I want two blankets tonight. (*Still not satisfied, he sends the old man sprawling with a shove. The old man crawls back laboriously to his seat.* BOESMAN *watches him, then hears* LENA *returning. He throws back the blanket.*) If you tell her, I'll kill you. "*Bulala wena!*" (*Returns to his shelter, sits down and continues drinking. He will remain in this position, watching* LENA *and the old man, until the end of the act.*)

LENA. (*A few small pieces of wood is all she has found.*) It's too dark now. (*Goes to the fire. Their tea is now ready. She pours it into two mugs, taking one of them and half the bread to* BOESMAN. *Then she joins the old man with her share. She sits beside him.*) As long as it doesn't rain it won't be so bad. The blanket will help. Nights are long, but they don't last forever. This wind will also get tired. (*Her mug of tea and bread are placed before them.*) It's a long time since we had somebody else with us. Sit close to the fire. That's it! (*Throws on another piece of wood.*) It won't last long, but it's big enough. Not much to see. This is all. This is mine. Look at this mug, *Outa* . . . old mug, hey? Bitter tea, a piece of bread. Bitter and brown. The bread should have bruises. It's my life. (*Passing him the mug.*) There, don't waste time. It's still warm. (*They drink and eat.* BOES-MAN *is watching them from the shelter, his bread and tea untouched before him.*)

CURTAIN

ACT TWO

An hour later.

LENA *and the old man are still sitting together on the box, huddled together under the blanket.* BOESMAN *is on his legs in front of them, the second bottle of wine in his hands. Under the influence of the wine his characteristic violence is now heightened by a wild excitability. His bread and tea are still untouched on the ground.*

BOESMAN. Again.

LENA. No.

BOESMAN. Yes!

LENA. You said that was the last time.

BOESMAN. You didn't do it right.

LENA. Have a heart, Boesman. Leave us alone now, man!

BOESMAN. Come on! "Please *my baasie!*" (*Pause.*) Lena!

LENA. (*Giving in.*) "Please *my baasie.*"

BOESMAN. Properly. The way you did it this morning.

LENA. "Please *my baasie.*"

BOESMAN. (*The old man.*) Him too. Hey!

LENA. Say it, *Outa.* (*The old man mumbles something.*)

OLD AFRICAN. *Nga bonga e baye. Nga funa ujwala.* (Thank you for the blanket. I want some wine.)

BOESMAN. "*Ag siestog my baas.*"

LENA. "*Ag siestog my baas.*"

BOESMAN. No bloody good.

LENA. (*Reaching breaking point, she jumps up.*) Enough, Boesman!

BOESMAN. Not enough. Whiteman won't feel sorry for you.

38

LENA. Then you try!

BOESMAN. You must make the words crawl to him, with your tongue between their back legs. Then when the *baas* looks at you, wag it just a little . . . *"Siestoggies my baas! Siestoggies my groot little baasie!"*

LENA. Whiteman! Whiteman! Whiteman's dog. *Voetsek!* (BOESMAN *laughs.*) I'll pick up a stone, Boesman. (BOESMAN *growls at her. Sitting down beside the old man again:*) That's what he is, *Outa.* Make life hell for anything that smells poor. He's worse. They stop barking when you've walked past. This one's following me to my grave.

BOESMAN. (*Launching into a vulgar parody of* LENA, *with the appropriate servile postures and gestures.*) "Just an old *Hotnot baas.* Lena *baas.* From old *Coega baas. Ja my baas."* (*Turns on her.*) You! (*Extends the pantomime to a crude imitation of the scene that morning when the Korsten shacks were demolished. Peering at something:*) "Boesman. Hey, Boesman! There's something strange coming our way. Save our things! (*In and out of the shelter.*) Give us time, my baas. Jesus, not again. Poor old Lena. Just one more load, baas. Poor old Lena!"* (*Abandoning the act and turning on* LENA *again.*) This morning! That's how you said it. That's what you looked like.

LENA. And did somebody feel sorry for us?

BOESMAN. The lot of you! Crawling out of your holes. Like worms. *Babalas* as the day you were born. That piece of ground was rotten with drunkies. Trying to save their rubbish, falling over each other . . . ! "Run, you bastards! Whiteman's bulldozer is chasing you!" (*Big laugh.*)

LENA. And then he hit me for dropping the empties.

BOESMAN. (*The bulldozer.*) Slowly it comes . . . slowly . . . big yellow *donner* with its jawbone on the ground. One bite and there's a hole in the earth! Whiteman on top. I watched him. He had to work old brother. Wasn't easy to tell that thing where to go. He had to work with those knobs! In reverse . . . take aim! . . . open jaws up! . . . then horse power in top gear and smashed to hell. One push and it was flat. All of them. Slum clearance! And what did we do? Stand and look. (*Another imitation.*) "*Haai!* Look. Whiteman is a strange bloody thing." (BOESMAN *laughs.*) But the dogs knew. They had their tails between their legs. They were ready to run.

LENA. He laughed then too, *Outa.* Like a madman. Running around shouting and laughing at our own people.

BOESMAN. So would you if you'd seen them.

LENA. I did.

BOESMAN. You didn't. You were sitting there with our things crying.

LENA. I saw myself.

BOESMAN. And what did that look like?

LENA. Me.

BOESMAN. Only one.

LENA. One's enough.

BOESMAN. Enough! Leave that word alone. You don't know what it means.

LENA. It was the same story for all of us. Once is enough if it's a sad one.

BOESMAN. Sad story? Those two that had the fight because somebody grabbed the wrong pants? The old one trying to catch his donkey? Or that other one running around with his porridge, looking for a fire to finish cooking it? It was motion pictures, man! And I watched it. Beginning to end, the way it happened. *I* saw it. *Me.* The women and children sitting there with their snot and tears. The *pondoks* falling. The men standing, looking, as the yellow *donner* pushed them over and then staring at the pieces when they were the only things left standing. I saw all that! The whiteman stopped the bulldozer and smoked a cigarette. I saw that too. (*Another act.*) "*Ek sê my baas* . . . !" He threw me the *stompie.* "*Dankie Baas.*"

LENA. They made a big pile and burnt everything.

BOESMAN. Bonfire!

LENA. He helped drag what was left of the *pondoks* . . .

BOESMAN. Of course. Full of disease. That one in the uniform told me. *"Dankie Baas!"*

LENA. Just like that.

BOESMAN. (*Violently.*) Yes! *Dankie Baas.* You should have said it too, sitting there with your sad story. Whiteman was doing us a favour. You should have helped him. He wasn't just burning *pondoks.* They alone can't stink like that. Or burn like that. There was something else in that fire, something rotten. Us! Our sad stories, our smells, our world! And it burnt, brother. It burnt. I watched that too. The end was a pile of ashes. And quiet. Then . . . Jesus! . . . then I went back to the place where our *pondok* had been. It was gone! You understand that? Gone! I wanted to call you and show you. There where we crawled in and out like baboons, where we used to sit like them and eat, our head between our knees, our fingers in the pot, hiding away so that the others wouldn't see our food. . . . I could stand there! There was room for me to stand straight. You know what that is? Listen now. I'm going to use a word. Freedom! *Ja,* I've heard them talk it. Freedom! That's what the whiteman gave us. I've got my feelings too, Sister. It was a big one I had when I stood there. That's why I laughed, why I was happy. When we picked up our things and started to walk I wanted to sing. It was Freedom!

LENA. You still got it, old *ding?* (BOESMAN *stares at her dumbly. He wanders around aimlessly, looking at the fire, the other two, the shelter, as if he were itemizing every detail in his present situation.* LENA *watches him.*) You lost it? (BOESMAN *doesn't answer.*) Your big word? That made you so happy?

BOESMAN. When I turned off the road, when I said Swartkops. I didn't want to! Say it, or think it. Any of the old places. I didn't want to. I tried! The world was open this morning. It was big! All the roads . . . new ways, new places. Jesus! It made me drunk. Which one?

When the traffic light said "Go" there at Berry's Corner I nearly kaked in my pants.

LENA. So that's what we were looking for, lost there in the back streets. Should have seen us, *Outa!* Down one, up the other, back to where we started from . . . looking for Boesman's Freedom.

BOESMAN. I had it! It was you with your big mouth and stupid questions. "Where we going?" Every corner! "Hey, Boesman, where we going?" "Let's try Veeplaas." "How about Coega?" All you could think of was those old rubbish dumps. "Bethelsdorp . . . Missionvale . . ." Don't listen to her, Boesman! Walk! "Redhouse . . . Kleinskool . . ." They were like fleas on my life. I scratched until I was raw.

LENA. We had to go somewhere. Couldn't walk around Korsten carrying your Freedom forever.

BOESMAN. Every time you opened your mouth it got worse.

LENA. Bad day for Lena. Three empties and Boesman's Freedom in pieces.

BOESMAN. By the time you shut-up we were just an old raggedy-ass and his bitch in the backyard of the world. I saw that piece of iron on the side of the road. I should have passed it. Gone on! Freedom's a long walk. But the sun was low. Our days are too short. (*Pause.*) Too late, Boesman. Too late for it today. Finish and *klaar.* Another *pondok.* (*Shouting violently.*) It's no use, *Baas.* Boesman's done it again. Bring your bulldozer tomorrow and push it over! (*To the old man.*) Then you must run. It will chase you too. *Sa! Sa vir die kaffer!*

LENA. Don't listen to him, *Outa.* There's no hurry. When it's over they let you walk away. Nobody had to run. One by one we went, a few things on the head, different ways, one by one.

BOESMAN. Whiteman's wasting his time trying to help us. Pushed it over this morning and here it is again. Push this one over and I'll do it somewhere else. Make another hole in the ground, crawl into it and live my life crooked.

One push. That's all we need. One push, into jail; one push, out of your job; one push and it's pieces. Must I tell you why? Listen! I'm thinking deep tonight. We're whiteman's rubbish. That's why he's so fed-up with us. He can't get rid of his rubbish. He throws it away, we pick it up. Wear it. Sleep in it. Eat it. We're made of it now. His rubbish is people.

LENA. Throw yourself away and leave us alone.

BOESMAN. It's been done. Why do you think we sit here like this? We've been thrown away. Rubbishes. Him too. (*The old man.*) They don't want him anymore. Useless. But there! You see what happens. Lena picks him up. Wraps him in a blanket. Gives him food.

LENA. You picked up yours. I picked up mine.

BOESMAN. I got mine for nothing. It made a *pondok*. What you going to do with him? (*Pause.*) Hey! I'm speaking to you. You paid a lot for that piece of turd. Bottle of wine. You happy now?

LENA. I didn't buy *Outa* for happiness.

BOESMAN. So then what's the use of him? Is he hot-stuff? Keeping you warm there?

LENA. No.

BOESMAN. You two up to something under that blanket? (LENA *doesn't answer.*) Lena and old better-than-nothing. Waiting for me to go to sleep, hey? Dirty things!

LENA. No, Boesman.

BOESMAN. You're cold, you're hungry, you're not making happiness, but still you want him.

LENA. Yes.

BOESMAN. (*Turning away with a forced laugh.*) O God! She's gone mad. Lena's gone mad on the mud flats. Sit there with a Kaffir . . . (*His laughter spirals up into violent bewilderment. He faces her savagely.*) Why! Why!!! (*Pause.*)

LENA. (*She takes her time.*) What we doing to you, Boesman? Why can't you leave us alone? You've had the wine, you've got the shelter. What else is there?

Me?! *Haai,* Boesman, is that why he worries you? You jealous . . . because Lena's turned you down, your *pondok* and your bottle? Must I tell you why? That's not a *pondok,* Boesman. (*The shelter.*) It's a coffin. All of them. You bury my life in your *pondoks.* Not tonight. Crawl into darkness and silence before I'm dead? No! I'm on this earth, not in it. Look now. (*She nudges the old man.*) Lena!

OLD AFRICAN. Lena.

LENA. *Ewe* Lena. (*To* BOESMAN.) That's me. You're right, Boesman. It's here and now. This is the time and place. To hell with the others. They're finished, and mixed up, anyway. I don't know why I'm here, how I got here. And you won't tell me. Doesn't matter. They've ended *now.* The walks led *here.* Tonight. And he sees it.

BOESMAN. What's there to see? Boesman and Lena on the mud flats at Swartkops. Like any other night.

LENA. That's right.

BOESMAN. And tomorrow night will be the same. What you going to do then? Maybe I'll kick you out again.

LENA. You didn't kick me out.

BOESMAN. Tomorrow night I will. And you'll sit alone. Because he won't be here. That I tell you. Or anybody else.

LENA. He's here now. (BOESMAN *leaves her and sits down in front of his shelter, drinking, in a withdrawn and violent silence. To the old man:*) Not yet, Outa. (*Shaking him.*) It's not finished. Open your eyes. (*To* BOESMAN.) If you don't want your bread and tea pass it this way, man. (BOESMAN *studies* LENA *in silence for a few seconds then stretches out a leg and pushes over the mug of tea. He watches* LENA *for a reaction. There is none. In a sudden fury he picks up the bread and hurls it into the darkness.*)

BOESMAN. I've told you, we've got no help. (*Disappears into the shelter with his bottle of wine, reappears, on his knees, almost immediately.*) I'm kicking you out *now.* Even if you change your mind you can't come in.

LENA. I won't, Boesman. (BOESMAN *disappears into the shelter.*) Maybe he'll sleep now. (*The old man leans forward.*) No, *Outa,* not us. (*Shaking him.*) Listen to me. You'll never sleep long enough. Sit close. *Ja! Hotnot* and a *Kaffir* got no time for apartheid on a night like this. We must keep that bit of wood for later. After that there's nothing left. Don't think about what you're feeling. Something else. Warm times. Let's talk about warm times. Good walk on a nice day! Not too long, not too hot. Otherwise you're back in hell again . . . as hot as this one's cold. In and out, hey, *Outa,* we poor people. But when it's just right! It's a feeling. And a taste, when you lick your lips. Dust and sweat. Hard work too. Watch tomorrow. You start to dig for prawns, your hands are stiff, the mud and water is cold, but after a little while you start to sweat and it's okay. *Outa* must help us dig tomorrow. Get nice and warm. And a good dance! Jesus, *Outa.* There's a warm feeling. If we had a *dop* inside now we could have tried. Hard to make party without a *dop.* (*Humming.*) Da . . . da . . . da. *Outa* know that one? Old *Hotnot* dance. Clap your hands. So. (*She starts clapping and singing softly.*) "*Die trane die rol vir jou bokkie!*" Coegakop days! Lena danced the moon down and the sun up. The parties, *Outa!* Happy Christmas, Happy New Year, Happy Birthday . . . all the Happies. We danced them. The sad ones too. Somebody born, somebody buried. We danced them in, we danced them out. It helps us forget. Few *dops* and a guitar and it's *voetsek* yesterday and to hell with tomorrow. (*Singing.*) Da . . . da . . . da . . . da . . . *Outa's* not clapping. So. (*Clapping and singing.*) Da . . . da . . . da . . . da . . .

> "A taste of Kondens Milk
> Makes life so sweet.
> Boesman is a Boesman
> Because he's all dark meat!"

Not like your dances. No war dances for us. They say we were slaves in the old days. Just your feet on the earth and then stamp. Hit it hard! (*Still seated, she demon-strates.*) Da . . . da . . . da . . . da . . . Nothing fancy. We don't tickle it like the white people. Maybe it laughs for them. It's a hard mother to us. So we dance hard. Let it feel us. Clap with me. (LENA *is now on her legs. Still clapping, she starts to dance. In the course of it* BOESMAN's *head appears in the opening to the shelter. He watches her. Speaking as she makes the first heavy steps:*) So for Korsten. So for the walk. So for Swartkops. *This* time. *Next* time. *Last* time. (*Singing.*)

> Korsten had its empties,
> Swartkops got its bait,
> Lena's got her bruises,
> 'Cause Lena's a *Hotnot* maid.

> Kleinskool got prickly pears,
> Missionvale's got salt,
> Lena's got a Boesman,
> So it's always Lena's fault.

> Coegakop is far away,
> Redhouse up the river,
> Lena's in the mud again,
> *Outa's* sitting with her.

(*She stops, breathing heavily, then wipes her forehead with her hand and licks one of the fingers.*) Sweat! You see, *Outa*. Sweat. Sit close now, I'm warm. You feel me? And we've still got that wood! (*They huddle together again under the blanket.* BOESMAN *is watching from the shelter. He lets them settle down before speaking.*)

BOESMAN. I dropped the empties. (LENA *looks at him, she doesn't understand.*) This morning. When we had to clear out of the *pondok.* I carried the sack. (*It takes* LENA *a long time.*) I dropped it.

LENA. (*Understands now. She speaks quietly.*) You said I did.

BOESMAN. Yes.

LENA. You blamed me. You hit me.

BOESMAN. Yes.

LENA. (*To the old man.*) He wanted to count the bottles before we left. Three were broken. He stopped hitting when the whitemen laughed. Took off his hat and smiled at them. "Just a old bitch, *Baas.*" They laughed louder. (*Her bruises.*) Too dark to see them now. He's hit me everywhere. (*Her arms open . . . looking down at her body. She has a sense of her frail anatomy. She feels herself.*) *Haai* Jesus! Look at it. Sagging tits, skinny ribs. (*Looks up at* BOESMAN. *He is still watching her from the shelter.*) For nothing then. Why do you tell me now? (*Pause—he stares at her.*) You want to hurt me again. Why, Boesman? I've come through a day that God can take back. Even if it was my last one. Isn't that enough for you? (*Pause.*) No. Why must you hurt me so much? What have I really done? Why didn't you hit yourself this morning? You broke the bottles. Or the whiteman that kicked us out? Why did you hit me?

BOESMAN. (*Now out of the shelter.*) Why do I hit you? (*Tries to work it out. He looks at his hands, clenches one and smashes it into the palm of the other.*) Why?

LENA. To keep your life warm? Learn to dance, Boesman. Leave your bruises on the earth.

BOESMAN. (*Another blow.*) Why?

LENA. (*Still quietly.*) Maybe you just want to touch me, to know I'm here. Try it the other way. Open your fist, put your hand on me. I'm here. I'm Lena.

BOESMAN. Lena! (*Another blow, the hardest. He looks at her and nods.*) Lena . . . and I'm Boesman.

LENA. Hit yourself!

BOESMAN. (*Holding up his palm.*) It doesn't hurt.

LENA. (*The first note of outrage.*) And when it's me? Does that hurt you? What have I done, Boesman? It's my life. Hit your own.

BOESMAN. (*Equally desperate, looking around dumbly.*) Show it to me! Where is it? This thing that happens to me. Where? Is it the *pondok?* Whiteman pushed it over this morning. Wind will do it to this one. The road I walked today? Behind us! Swartkops? Next week it's somewhere else. The wine? Bottles are empty. Where is it!!! (*Pause.*) I look, and I see you. I listen, I hear you.

LENA. And when you hit . . . ?

BOESMAN. You. You cry.

LENA. You hear that too?

BOESMAN. Yes.

LENA. (*Now almost inarticulate with outrage.*) Jesus! Jesus! *Outa* hear all that? Hey! (*She shakes him violently.*) You can't sleep now! (*Changing her tone, pleading.*) Please, *Outa*. Just a little bit longer. I'll put the wood on the fire. (*Does so.*) Wake up. This is the truth now. Listen.

BOESMAN. (*Watching her.*) You have gone mad tonight.

LENA. He's got to listen!

BOESMAN. He doesn't know what you're saying. *You* must wake up! You've wasted your time with him. You've been talking to yourself tonight the way you've been talking to yourself your whole life. You're dumb. When you make a hole in your face the noise that comes out is as good as nothing, because nobody hears it.

LENA. Say it in the Kaffir tongue. "You hit me for nothing." Say it!

BOESMAN. No.

LENA. Then let him see it. (*Crawls to* BOESMAN *in an attitude of abject beggary.*) Hit me. Please, Boesman. For a favour. My last one, s'truesgod. Hit me now. (*To the old man.*) I've shown you the bruises. Now watch. (*Pause . . .* BOESMAN *is staring at her with disgust.*) What you waiting for? You don't need reasons. Let him see it. Hit me!

BOESMAN. (*Withering disgust.*) Shit.

LENA. Who?

BOESMAN. SHIT!

LENA. Me? (*This is too much for* LENA; *she wanders around vacantly, almost as if she were drunk.*) Dear

God! Dear, dear, dear, dear God! I've got the bruises . . .
he did it, he broke the bottles, but I've got the bruises
and it's "Shit" to me? What have I done?

BOESMAN. He doesn't know what you're saying!

LENA. Look at me, *Outa* . . . Lena! Me.

BOESMAN. There's only me. All you've got is me and
I'm saying "Shit!"

LENA. (*Beside the old man on the box . . . softly . . .*)
Outa?

BOESMAN. You think I haven't got secrets in my heart
too? That's mine. Shit! Small little word, hey. Shit. But
it fits. (*Parodying himself.*) *"Ja baas! Dankie baas!"*
Shit, Boesman! And you? Don't ask me what you've
done. Just look. You say you can see yourself. Take a
good look tonight! Crying for a bottle, begging for
bruises. Shit, Lena! Boesman and Lena, shit! We're not
people anymore. Freedom's not for us. We stood there
under the sky . . . two crooked *Hotnots*. So they
laughed. Shit, World! All there is to say. That's our
word. After that our life is dumb. Like your womb. All
that came out of it was silence. There should have been
noise. You pushed out silence. And Boesman buried it.
Took the spade the next morning and pushed our hope
back into the dirt. Deep holes! When I filled them up I
said it again: Shit. One day your turn. One day mine.
Two more holes somewhere. The earth will puke when
they push us in. And then it's finished. The end of Boesman and Lena. That's all it is, tonight or any other
night. Two dead *Hotnots* living together. And you want
him to look? To see? He must close his eyes. That's
what I'll say for you in the Kaffir-tongue. *Musa
khangela!* Don't look! That's what you must tell him.
Musa khangela!

LENA. He can't hear you, Boesman.

BOESMAN. *Musa khangela!*

LENA. Don't shout. I'm alone.

BOESMAN. What do you mean?

LENA. He can't hear you.

BOESMAN. Then wake him up.

LENA. Does it look like sleep? *Outa's* closed his eyes. The old thing must have been tired. I tried to keep them open, make him look. When he closed them his darkness was mine. (*Pause . . .* BOESMAN *now realizes.* LENA *looks up at him.*) *Ja,* he's dead.

BOESMAN. How do you know?

LENA. He let go. He was holding my hand. He grabbed it, held it tight, then he let go.

BOESMAN. Feel his heart.

LENA. He's dead, Boesman. His hand is empty.

BOESMAN. (*Unbelievingly.*) He didn't cry, or something . . .

LENA. Maybe it wasn't worth it.

BOESMAN. *He* wasn't worth it. Bottle of wine! And now . . . ? Didn't last you long. (*The bottle in his hand.*) Mine too. Finished. (*Throws the bottle aside.*) There goes mine. (*Pause—he looks at* LENA *and the old man again.*) Stone-dead?

LENA. *Ja.*

BOESMAN. (*Walking away.*) All yours.

LENA. Help me put him down.

BOESMAN. (*Quickly.*) He's got nothing to do with me. (*Sits down in front of his shelter, nervous and uncertain.*) You wanted him. You called him to the fire.

LENA. (*Gently easing the body down.*) Hey, heavy! No wonder we get tired. It's not just the things on your head. There's also yourself. (*Moves away.*)

BOESMAN. (*After a pause.*) And now? What's going to happen now?

LENA. Is something going to happen now?

BOESMAN. Dead man.

LENA. Only a *Kaffir. Outa.* Didn't even learn his real name. He said mine so nicely. Sorry, old *ding.* Sorry.

BOESMAN. (*False indifference.*) *Ja,* well . . . tomorrow is another day. I'm tired. Low water early. We'll have to hustle if we want prawns. I'm going to sleep. (*Pause.*) I said I'm going to sleep.

LENA. I heard you.

BOESMAN. (*Before disappearing into the shelter.*) He's got nothing to do with me.

LENA. "Tomorrow is another day." Maybe, hey, *Outa.* Maybe. So that's all. Hold on for as long as you can, and then let go.

BOESMAN. (*Shouting from inside the shelter.*) What are you doing?

LENA. Put your hands on the things in your life. Yours were full. Mug of tea, piece of bread. . . . Me. Somebody else. Touch them, hold them . . .

BOESMAN. (*His head appearing in the opening of the shelter.*) What you doing?

LENA. (*Looking at him.*) . . . or make a fist and hit them.

BOESMAN. You can't just sit there. You better do something. (*Pause.*) Listen to me, Lena!

LENA. Why must I listen to you?

BOESMAN. (*Coming out.*) This is no time for more bloody nonsense! It's serious.

LENA. When *you* want somebody to listen, it's serious.

BOESMAN. That! (*Pointing to the body.*)

LENA. *Outa* still worry you? Haai, Boesman. He's dead.

BOESMAN. Dead men are dangerous. You better get rid of it.

LENA. Real piece of rubbish now, hey. What must I do?

BOESMAN. I don't give a damn. Just do it.

LENA. How do you throw away a dead *Kaffir?*

BOESMAN. Your problems. He's got nothing . . .

LENA. . . . to do with you. Go back to sleep, Boesman.

BOESMAN. I am! Why must I worry? I did nothing. Clear conscience! Come and do his nonsense here! This is my place. I was here first. He should have stayed with his own sort. Then when I wanted to get rid of him, *you* stopped me. (*There is no response from* LENA *to* BOES-

MAN'S *growing agitation. This provokes him even more.*)
Are you a bloody fool?

LENA. You say so.

BOESMAN. That's big trouble lying there.

LENA. His troubles are over.

BOESMAN. And ours? What do you think is going to
happen tomorrow?

LENA. I don't care.

BOESMAN. Well, I'm just warning you, you better have
answers ready. Dead man! There's going to be questions.

LENA. About him? About rubbish? Hey, hey, hey!
Outa, hear that. Tomorrow is a special day. They're going
to ask questions! About you! Hot stuff, hey. "What's his
name?" "Where's he come from?"

BOESMAN. Never saw him before in my life!

LENA. "Who did it?"

BOESMAN. (*Sharply.*) Did what? He died by himself.

LENA. Too bad you can't tell them, *Outa.*

BOESMAN. I did nothing.

LENA. Why don't they ask some questions when we're
alive?

BOESMAN. (*Interrupting her.*) Hey! You saw.

LENA. What did I see?

BOESMAN. I did nothing to him. You saw that.

LENA. Now you want a witness too.

BOESMAN. I didn't touch him. You tell them.

LENA. What?

BOESMAN. The truth.

LENA. You got some words tonight, Boesman. Freedom.
Truth. What's that? Shit?

BOESMAN. Stop your jokes, Lena! When they come tomorrow you just tell them. I was minding my own busi-
ness. I only come here to dig for prawns.

LENA. Teach me again, Boesman. You really know how
the whiteman likes to hear it. "He's jus' a *Hotnot, Baas.*
Wasn't doing any harm." How's that? Will that make
him feel sorry for you?

BOESMAN. Then the *Kaffir* came. And *you* called him to the fire.

LENA. *"Siestoggies my baas."*

BOESMAN. I didn't want him. I didn't touch him.

LENA. "Boesman didn't want him, *baas*."

BOESMAN. I hate *Kaffirs*.

LENA. "He hates *Kaffirs, baas*."

BOESMAN. NO!!

LENA. "He loves *Kaffirs,* baas."

BOESMAN. God, Lena! (*Grabs a bottle and moves violently towards her. He stops himself in time. LENA has made no move to escape or protect herself.*)

LENA. *Ja,* got to be careful now. There's one already. (*BOESMAN is now very frightened. LENA watches him.*) Whiteman's dog, his tail between his legs because the *baas* is going to be cross. Jesus! We crawl, hey. You're right, Boesman. And beg. "Give us a chance." *Siestog. I'm* sorry for you. Hey. Maybe he's not dead. (*BOESMAN looks at her.*) That's a thought, hey! Maybe he's not dead, and everything is still okay.

BOESMAN. You said he was.

LENA. You believe me? You mean you're listening to Lena tonight? Are we talking to each other?

BOESMAN. Is he dead?

(*LENA laughs softly. BOESMAN moves uncertainly towards the body, unable to ignore the possibility with which she is tormenting him. He looks down at the dead man.*)

LENA. Go on.

BOESMAN. Wake up!

LENA. Doesn't speak our language, remember.

BOESMAN. Hey!

LENA. That's better.

BOESMAN. (*Nudging the body with his foot.*) *Vuka!*

LENA. Didn't he move there? Imagine he stands up now? Happy days! Dig prawns tomorrow, buy another bottle, give me a hiding. (BOESMAN *is hesitating, uncertain of what to do next.*) Feel his heart. (*The nudge becomes a kick.*) Much better. Let him feel your foot.

BOESMAN. Get up!

LENA. Don't let him play stupid with you. Make him get up. Tell him to go.

BOESMAN. *Voetsek!*

LENA. Louder! These *Kaffirs* are cheeky.

BOESMAN. (*His violence building up—another kick.*) Go die in your own world! (*Pause.* BOESMAN, *rigid with anger and hatred, stares down at the inert body.*)

LENA. No bloody good. He's dead. And you, old brother, you're in trouble!

BOESMAN. (*His control breaking.*) Bloody fool! (*Falls to his knees and beats the body violently with his fists.* LENA *watches in silence. When* BOESMAN *is finished he goes back to his place in front of the shelter.*)

LENA. So that's how you do it. I know what it feels like. Now I know what it looks like. What do you think about, in between, when you rest? Where to hit next? (BOESMAN *is breathing heavily*.) Hard work to beat the daylights out like that. Too bad there wasn't any left in him. *Outa's* in darkness. He won't be sore tomorrow, sit and count his bruises in the light. But he'll have them. When you hit me I go blue. (*Pause.*) You shouldn't have hit him, Boesman. Those bruises! Fingerprints. Yours. On him. You've made it worse for yourself. Dead *Kaffir* and a *Hotnot* bitch with bruises . . . and Boesman sitting nearby with no skin on his knuckles. What's that look like? The answer to all their questions. They won't even ask them now. They'll just grab you . . . (*Carefully . . .*) . . . for something you didn't do! That's the worst. When you didn't do it. Like the hiding you gave me for dropping the empties. Now you'll know what it feels like. You were clever to tell me. It hurt more than your fists. You know where you feel that one? Inside. Where your fists can't reach. A bruise there! Now it's your turn!

(BOESMAN, *barely controlling his growing panic, gets
   stiffly to his legs. He looks around . . . the dead
   man,* LENA, *the darkness . . . then makes up his
   mind and starts to collect their things together.*)

BOESMAN. Come! (LENA *doesn't respond.*) On your
legs! We're going.
   LENA. *Haai,* Boesman! This hour? Where? (BOES-
MAN *doesn't answer.*) You don't know again, do you?
Just crawl around looking for a way out of your life.
Why must I go with you? Because you're Boesman and
I'm Lena?
   BOESMAN. (*Urgently packing up their belongings . . .
rolling blanket up.*) Are you coming? It's the last time I
ask you.
   LENA. No. The first time I tell you. No. I've walked
with you a long way, old *ding!* It's finished now. Here,
in the Swartkops mud. I wanted to finish it this morning,
sitting there on the pavement. That was the word in my
mouth. NO! Enough! I wasn't ready for it yet. I am
now. (BOESMAN *is staring at her.*) Don't you understand? It's over. Look at you! Look at your hands! Fists
again. When Boesman doesn't understand something, he
hits it. You didn't understand him (the dead man), did
you? I chose him! A *Kaffir!* Then he goes and buggers-up
everything by dying. So you hit him. And now me. No,
Boesman! I'm not going with you! You want to hit me,
don't you? (*Barely controlling his panic now,* BOESMAN
goes on packing.) Run! It's trouble. Life's showing you
bullets again. So run. But this time you run alone. When
you think you're safe don't rest and wait for me to find
you. I'm not running at all. I'm tired. When you're gone
I'll crawl in there and sleep. (BOESMAN *stops his packing
and looks up at* LENA. *He realizes her intention.*)
   BOESMAN. That's what you think! (*Starts to smash the
shelter with methodical and controlled violence.*)
   LENA. *Hotnot* bulldozer! Hey, hey! (*Jumps to her*

legs and prances around.) *Dankie Baas,* Boesman! Smash
it to hell! This is my laugh. Run, you old bastard. Whiteman's chasing you!

BOESMAN. (*The shelter is totally demolished. He col-
lects their things together with renewed energy.*) Don't
think I'm leaving you anything.

LENA. (*Pursuing him ruthlessly.*) Take the lot! (*Help-
ing him collect it all together.*) This . . . this. . . .
Don't forget my blanket. (*It is still wrapped around the
dead man.* BOESMAN *hesitates.*) You frightened? There!
(*Pulls it off and throws it at* BOESMAN.) Everything! I
want nothing at all. It's my life, but I don't want to feel
it anymore. I've held on tight too long. I want to let go.
I want nothing! What's your big word? Freedom! Tonight it's Freedom for Lena. Whiteman gave you yours
this morning, but you lost it. Must I tell you how? When
you put all that on your back. There wasn't room for it
as well. (*All their belongings are now collected together
in a pile.*) You should have thrown it on the bonfire.
And me with it. You should have walked away naked!
That's what I'm going to be now. Naked. The noise I
make now is going to be new. Maybe I'll cry . . . or
laugh? I want to laugh as well. I feel light. Get ready,
Boesman. When you walk I'm going to laugh! At you!
(BOESMAN *is loading himself up with their belongings
. . . blankets, mattress, boxes. It is a difficult operation,
the bundles are awkward, things keep falling out. But he
finally manages to get it all on his back and under his
arms. He stands before* LENA *a grotesquely overburdened
figure.*) *Eina!* Look at you. Jesus, Boesman, the road's
going to be long tomorrow. And hard. You'll sweat. What
way you walking? Veeplaas? Follow the sun, that's
where it goes. Sand between your toes tomorrow night.
(*Violently.*) So what you waiting for? Can't we say goodbye? We'll have to do it one day. It's not forever. Come
on. Let's say it now. Goodbye! Okay, now go. Go!!
Walk!! (LENA *turns her back on him violently and walks*

away. BOESMAN *stands motionless. She ends up beside the old man.*) *Outa,* why the hell you do it so soon? There's things I didn't tell you, man. And now this as well. It's still happening! (*Softly.*) . . . O my God. Can't throw yourself away before your time. Hey, *Outa.* Even you had to wait for it. (*Gets up slowly and goes to* BOESMAN.) Give! (*He passes over the bucket.*) Hasn't got a hole in it yet. Might be whiteman's rubbish, but I can still use it. (*It goes on to her head.*) Where we going? Better be far. Coegakop. That's our farthest. That's where we started.

BOESMAN. Coega to Veeplaas.

LENA. (*Slowly loading up the rest of her share.*) First walk. I always remember that one. It's the others.

BOESMAN. (*As* LENA *loads.*) Veeplaas to Redhouse. On *baas* Robbie's place.

LENA. "My God," old *baas* Robbie.

BOESMAN. Redhouse to Missionvale . . . I worked on the salt pans. Missionvale to Bethelsdorp. Back again to Redhouse . . . that's where the child died. Then to Kleinskool. Kleinskool to Veeplaas. Veeplaas to here. First time. After that, Redhouse, *baas* Robbie was dead. Bethelsdorp, Korsten, Veeplaas, back here the second time. Then Missionvale again, Veeplaas, Korsten, and then here, now.

LENA. (*Pause . . . she is loaded.*) Is that the way it was? How I got here?

BOESMAN. Yes.

LENA. Truly?

BOESMAN. Yes. (*Pause.*)

LENA. It doesn't explain anything.

BOESMAN. I know.

LENA. Anyway, somebody saw a little bit. Dog and a dead man. (*They are ready to go.*) I'm alive, Boesman. There's daylights left in me. You still got a chance. Don't lose it. Next time you want to kill me, do it. Really do it. When you hit, hit those lights out. Don't be too late.

Do it yourself. Don't let the old bruises put the rope around your neck. Okay. But not so fast. It's dark. (*They look around for the last time, then turn and walk off into the darkness.*)

CURTAIN

GLOSSARY of Afrikaans (South African Dutch) words and phrases left untranslated in the text of this play

Aikona!—African vernacular meaning "No!"
babalas—hungover
baas, baasie—"Master" and its diminutive
Dè!—"There!," "Take it!"
dop—"drink" (as in "Have a drink!") Equivalent of English "tot"
Eina!—Exclamation of pain.
Ewe!—African vernacular meaning "Yes!"
gebabbel—babble
Haai!—Exclamation of surprise
hond—dog
Hotnot—indigenous African tribe
klap—a punch or a blow
lawaai—noise
Outa—old man
pondok, pondokkie—shelter, shanty
Sommer—only
stompie—cigarette butt
vastrap—dance
veld—countryside
Voetsek!—Get away!
"Ag siestog my baas"
"Siestoggies my baas" } "Oh, please my master"
"Siestoggies my groot (little) baasie!"
"Ek se ou pêllie"—"Hey there, buddy!"
"(Finish) en klaar"—Finished
"Môre, Baas!"—"Morning, Master!"
"Ek se!"—"Hey there!"
"Sa! Sa vir die kaffer!"—"Catch the nigger!"
"Die trane die rol vir jou bokkie!"—"I'm crying for you, baby!"
"Vat jou goed en trek!"—"Take your things and go!"

PROPERTY PLOT

ONSTAGE:
Refrigerator door—D. R. corner
Corrugated—U. C. behind rock
Bundle of 2 x 4 beam, 2 pieces moulding—U. C. on ramp
Fire pot—U. C. on ramp

OFF STAGE:
Truck door—*off* U. L. above
VW bonnet—*off* D. C.
Washtub—*off*
Large stick—*off*

BOESMAN:
Pack frame holding:
1 rolled blanket with 2 bottles wine
1 mattress
3 pieces burlap (used on roof of pondok)
1 long coil clothesline
1 box containing frypan, bait tin, 2 pieces burlap (sides of pondok), blanket
Center front support stick for pondok
Umbrella
Club
2 pieces cardboard with stiffeners
4 short pieces clothesline stuck in belt
Pocketknife, 4 clothespins, handkerchief—all in pockets
Tin of cigarettes
Tin of matches

LENA:
1 box containing:
Paraffin tin
Water bottle
Kettle, containing packet of bread, of tea
Enamel pan
Copper mug
Green mug
Aluminum pan
Rag
Bundle of firewood
Colored cloth
Head-ring (cloth wound like a doughnut, used to support box on top of head)

60

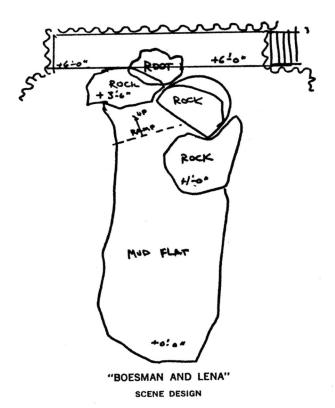

"BOESMAN AND LENA"
SCENE DESIGN